A GIFT FOR: _____

FROM:_____

Bible Promises for You
Copyright © 2016 by Zondervan

Requests for information should be addressed to:
Zondervan, 3900 Sparks Dr., SE, Grand Rapids, MI 49546

ISBN 978-0-310-09205-6

18 19 20 21 22 /QUAD/ 17 16 15 14 13 12 11 10 9 8 7 6 5 4 3 2

BIBLE
PROMISES
FOR YOU

New International Version

Every promise has
been fulfilled; not
one has failed.

JOSHUA 23:14

TABLE OF CONTENTS

ACCOMPLISHMENT

I have fought the good fight, I have finished
the race, I have kept the faith. Now there is in
store for me the crown of righteousness, which
the Lord, the righteous Judge, will award to me
on that day—and not only to me, but also to
all who have longed for his appearing.

2 Timothy 4:7-8

But whatever were gains to me I now consider
loss for the sake of Christ. What is more,
I consider everything a loss because of the
surpassing worth of knowing Christ Jesus my
Lord, for whose sake I have lost all things.
I consider them garbage, that I may gain
Christ and be found in him, not having a
righteousness of my own that comes from the
law, but that which is through faith in Christ—
the righteousness that comes from God on the
basis of faith.

Philippians 3:7-9

Lord, you establish peace for us;
all that we have accomplished you have
done for us.

Isaiah 26:12

A longing fulfilled is a tree of life.

Proverbs 13:12

ACCOMPLISHMENT

Each of them may eat and drink, and find satisfaction in all their toil—this is the gift of God.

ECCLESIASTES 3:13

You will eat the fruit of your labor;
blessings and prosperity will be yours.

PSALM 128:2

The LORD your God will make you most prosperous in all the work of your hands and in the fruit of your womb, the young of your livestock and the crops of your land. The LORD will again delight in you and make you prosperous, just as he delighted in your ancestors.

DEUTERONOMY 30:9

ANSWERED PRAYER

"In that day you will no longer ask me anything very truly. I tell you, my Father will give you whatever you ask in my name. Until now you have not asked for anything in my name. Ask and you will receive, and your joy will be complete."

JOHN 16:23-24

"They will not labor in vain,
    nor will they bear children doomed to
        misfortune;
for they will be a people blessed by the LORD,
    they and their descendants with them.
Before they call I will answer;
    while they are still speaking I will hear."

ISAIAH 65:23-24

This is the confidence we have in approaching God: that if we ask anything according to his will, he hears us. And if we know that he hears us—whatever we ask—we know that we have what we asked of him.

1 JOHN 5:14-15

ANSWERED PRAYER

In my distress I called to the LORD,
   and he answered me.
From deep in the realm of the dead I called
     for help,
   and you listened to my cry.

JONAH 2:2

The LORD is near to all who call on him,
   to all who call on him in truth.
He fulfills the desires of those who fear him;
   he hears their cry and saves them.

PSALM 145:18-19

[God] will respond to the prayer of the destitute;
   he will not despise their plea.
Let this be written for a future generation,
   that a people not yet created may praise
     the LORD.

PSALM 102:17-18

"Call to me and I will answer you and tell
you great and unsearchable things you do not
know."

JEREMIAH 33:3

ASSURANCE

Faith is confidence in what we hope for and assurance about what we do not see.

HEBREWS 11:1

I am convinced that neither death nor life, neither angels nor demons, neither the present nor the future, nor any powers, neither height nor depth, nor anything else in all creation, will be able to separate us from the love of God that is in Christ Jesus our Lord.

ROMANS 8:38-39

"Though the mountains be shaken
*   and the hills be removed,*
yet my unfailing love for you will not be shaken
*   nor my covenant of peace be removed,"*
says the LORD, who has compassion on you.

ISAIAH 54:10

"My sheep listen to my voice; I know them, and they follow me. I give them eternal life, and they shall never perish; no one will snatch them out of my hand. My Father, who has given them to me, is greater than all; no one can snatch them out of my Father's hand."

JOHN 10:27-29

ASSURANCE

Those who have served well gain an excellent standing and great assurance in their faith in Christ Jesus.

1 TIMOTHY 3:13

This is no cause for shame, because I know whom I have believed, and am convinced that he is able to guard what I have entrusted to him until that day.

2 TIMOTHY 1:12

Brothers and sisters, since we have confidence to enter the Most Holy Place by the blood of Jesus … let us draw near to God with a sincere heart and with the full assurance that faith brings, having our hearts sprinkled to cleanse us from a guilty conscience and having our bodies washed with pure water.

HEBREWS 10:19, 22

This is the confidence we have in approaching God: that if we ask anything according to his will, he hears us. And if we know that he hears us—whatever we ask—we know that we have what we asked of him.

1 JOHN 5:14-15

BELIEF

"God so loved the world that he gave his one and only Son, that whoever believes in him shall not perish but have eternal life."

JOHN 3:16

"Very truly I tell you, the one who believes has eternal life."

JOHN 6:47

If you declare with your mouth, "Jesus is Lord," and believe in your heart that God raised him from the dead, you will be saved. For it is with your heart that you believe and are justified, and it is with your mouth that you profess your faith and are saved.

ROMANS 10:9-10

Jesus said to her, "I am the resurrection and the life. The one who believes in me will live, even though they die; and whoever lives by believing in me will never die. Do you believe this?"

JOHN 11:25-26

Believe in the Lord Jesus, and you will be saved—you and your household.

ACTS 16:31

BELIEF

"Whoever believes in [Jesus] is not condemned."
JOHN 3:18

All the prophets testify about [Jesus] that everyone who believes in him receives forgiveness of sins through his name.
ACTS 10:43

To all who received [Jesus], to those who believed in his name, he gave the right to become children of God.
JOHN 1:12

Jesus told him, "Because you have seen me, you have believed; blessed are those who have not seen and yet have believed."
JOHN 20:29

Without faith it is impossible to please God, because anyone who comes to him must believe that he exists and that he rewards those who earnestly seek him.
HEBREWS 11:6

BLESSINGS

Blessed is the one
    who does not walk in step with the wicked
or stand in the way that sinners take
    or sit in the company of mockers,
but whose delight is in the law of the LORD,
    and who meditates on his law day and
        night.

PSALM 1:1-2

"Blessed is the one who trusts in the LORD,
    whose confidence is in him."

JEREMIAH 17:7

Praise be to the God and Father of our Lord
Jesus Christ, who has blessed us in the heavenly
realms with every spiritual blessing in Christ.

EPHESIANS 1:3

How abundant are the good things
    that you have stored up for those who fear
        you,
that you bestow in the sight of all,
    on those who take refuge in you.

PSALM 31:19

BLESSINGS

There is no difference between Jew and Gentile—the same Lord is Lord of all and richly blesses all who call on him, for, "Everyone who calls on the name of the Lord will be saved."

ROMANS 10:12-13

Every good and perfect gift is from above, coming down from the Father of the heavenly lights, who does not change like shifting shadows.

JAMES 1:17

Blessed are those you choose
    and bring near to live in your courts!
We are filled with the good things of
        your house,
    of your holy temple.

PSALM 65:4

"Blessed are the poor in spirit,
    for theirs is the kingdom of heaven."

MATTHEW 5:3

CHARITY

Blessed is the one who is kind to the needy.
PROVERBS 14:21

Blessed are those who have regard for the weak;
*   the LORD delivers them in times of trouble.*
The LORD protects and preserves them—
*   they are counted among the blessed in*
*   the land—*
*   he does not give them over to the desire of*
*   their foes.*
PSALM 41:1-2

Those who give to the poor will lack nothing,
*   but those who close their eyes to them*
*   receive many curses.*
PROVERBS 28:7

Whoever is kind to the poor lends to the LORD,
*   and he will reward them for what they*
*   have done.*
PROVERBS 19:17

The King will reply, "Truly I tell you, whatever you did for one of the least of these brothers and sisters of mine, you did for me."
MATTHEW 25:40

CHARITY

A generous person will prosper;
  whoever refreshes others will be refreshed.

PROVERBS 11:25

"If anyone gives even a cup of cold water to
one of these little ones who is my disciple,
truly I tell you, that person will certainly not
lose their reward."

MATTHEW 10:42

"But when you give a banquet, invite the poor,
the crippled, the lame, the blind, and you will
be blessed. Although they cannot repay you,
you will be repaid at the resurrection of the
righteous."

LUKE 14:13-14

Each of you should give what you have decided
in your heart to give, not reluctantly or under
compulsion, for God loves a cheerful giver.

2 CORINTHIANS 9:7

CHILDREN

Children are a heritage from the Lord,
offspring a reward from him.
Like arrows in the hands of a warrior
are children born in one's youth.
Blessed is the man
whose quiver is full of them.

PSALM 127:3-5

Start children off on the way they should go,
and even when they are old they will not
turn from it.

PROVERBS 22:6

Discipline your children, and they will give
you peace;
they will bring you the delights you desire.

PROVERBS 29:17

I have no greater joy than to hear that my
children are walking in the truth.

3 JOHN 1:4

"Whoever takes the lowly position of this child
is the greatest in the kingdom of heaven."

MATTHEW 18:4

CHILDREN

Fix these words of mine in your hearts and minds; tie them as symbols on your hands and bind them on your foreheads. Teach them to your children, talking about them when you sit at home and when you walk along the road, when you lie down and when you get up. Write them on the doorframes of your houses and on your gates, so that your days and the days of your children may be many in the land the LORD swore to give your ancestors, as many as the days that the heavens are above the earth.

DEUTERONOMY 11:18-21

Peter replied, "Repent and be baptized, every one of you, in the name of Jesus Christ for the forgiveness of your sins. And you will receive the gift of the Holy Spirit. The promise is for you and your children and for all who are far off—for all whom the Lord our God will call."

ACTS 2:38-39

CHILDREN OF GOD

"I will be a Father to you,
*   and you will be my sons and daughters,"*
says the Lord Almighty.

2 Corinthians 6:18

The Spirit himself testifies with our spirit that we are God's children.

Romans 8:16

Because you are sons, God sent the Spirit of his Son into our hearts, the Spirit who calls out, *"Abba,* Father." So you are no longer a slave, but God's child; and since you are his child, God has made you also an heir.

Galatians 4:6-7

For those who are led by the Spirit of God are the children of God. The Spirit you received does not make you slaves, so that you live in fear again; rather, the Spirit you received brought about your adoption to sonship. And by him we cry, *"Abba,* Father."

Romans 8:14-15

CHILDREN OF GOD

What great love the Father has lavished on us, that we should be called children of God! And that is what we are! The reason the world does not know us is that it did not know him.

1 JOHN 3:1

Follow God's example, therefore, as dearly loved children and walk in the way of love, just as Christ loved us and gave himself up for us as a fragrant offering and sacrifice to God.

EPHESIANS 5:1-2

So in Christ Jesus you are all children of God through faith. ... There is neither Jew nor Gentile, neither slave nor free, nor is there male and female, for you are all one in Christ Jesus.

GALATIANS 3:26, 28

Dear friends, now we are children of God, and what we will be has not yet been made known. But we know that when Christ appears, we shall be like him, for we shall see him as he is.

1 JOHN 3:2

CHRIST'S RETURN

Christ was sacrificed once to take away the sins of many; and he will appear a second time, not to bear sin, but to bring salvation to those who are waiting for him.

HEBREWS 9:28

"My Father's house has many rooms; if that were not so, would I have told you that I am going there to prepare a place for you? And if I go and prepare a place for you, I will come back and take you to be with me that you also may be where I am."

JOHN 14:2-3

"Men of Galilee," they said, "why do you stand here looking into the sky? This same Jesus, who has been taken from you into heaven, will come back in the same way you have seen him go into heaven."

ACTS 1:11

Look, he is coming with the clouds,
and every eye will see him.

REVELATION 1:7

CHRIST'S RETURN

The Lord himself will come down from heaven, with a loud command, with the voice of the archangel and with the trumpet call of God, and the dead in Christ will rise first.

1 THESSALONIANS 4:16

"Look, I am coming soon! My reward is with me, and I will give to each person according to what they have done."

REVELATION 22:12

The day of the Lord will come like a thief. The heavens will disappear with a roar; the elements will be destroyed by fire, and the earth and everything done in it will be laid bare.

2 PETER 3:10

"You also must be ready, because the Son of Man will come at an hour when you do not expect him."

LUKE 12:40

"This gospel of the kingdom will be preached in the whole world as a testimony to all nations, and then the end will come."

MATTHEW 24:14

CHURCH

You are a chosen people, a royal priesthood, a holy nation, God's special possession, that you may declare the praises of him who called you out of darkness into his wonderful light.

1 PETER 2:9

God's household … is the church of the living God, the pillar and foundation of the truth.

1 TIMOTHY 3:15

[Christ] is the head of the body, the church; he is the beginning and the firstborn from among the dead, so that in everything he might have the supremacy.

COLOSSIANS 1:18

Not giving up meeting together, as some are in the habit of doing, but encouraging one another—and all the more as you see the Day approaching.

HEBREWS 10:25

CHURCH

Let the message of Christ dwell among you richly as you teach and admonish one another with all wisdom through psalms, hymns, and songs from the Spirit, singing to God with gratitude in your hearts.

COLOSSIANS 3:16

They devoted themselves to the apostles' teaching and to fellowship, to the breaking of bread and to prayer. Everyone was filled with awe at the many wonders and signs performed by the apostles. All the believers were together and had everything in common. They sold property and possessions to give to anyone who had need. Every day they continued to meet together in the temple courts. They broke bread in their homes and ate together with glad and sincere hearts, praising God and enjoying the favor of all the people. And the Lord added to their number daily those who were being saved.

ACTS 2:42-47

COMFORT

Praise be to the God and Father of our Lord
Jesus Christ, the Father of compassion and the
God of all comfort, who comforts us in all our
troubles, so that we can comfort those in any
trouble with the comfort we ourselves receive
from God.

2 CORINTHIANS 1:3-4

"The LORD your God is with you,
the Mighty Warrior who saves.
He will take great delight in you;
in his love he will no longer rebuke you,
but will rejoice over you with singing."

ZEPHANIAH 3:17

The LORD is close to the brokenhearted
and saves those who are crushed in spirit.

PSALM 34:18

The Lamb at the center of the throne will be
their shepherd;
he will lead them to springs of living water.
And God will wipe away every tear from
their eyes.

REVELATION 7:17

COMFORT

Let the beloved of the LORD rest secure in him,
for he shields him all day long,
and the one the LORD loves rests between
his shoulders.

DEUTERONOMY 33:12

"I have seen their ways, but I will heal them;
I will guide them and restore comfort to
Israel's mourners,
creating praise on their lips.
Peace, peace, to those far and near,"
says the LORD. "And I will heal them."

ISAIAH 57:18-19

"Then young women will dance and be glad,
young men and old as well.
I will turn their mourning into gladness;
I will give them comfort and joy instead
of sorrow."

JEREMIAH 31:13

COMPASSION

You are a forgiving God, gracious and compassionate, slow to anger and abounding in love.

NEHEMIAH 9:17

The LORD is good to all;
he has compassion on all he has made.

PSALM 145:9

The LORD longs to be gracious to you;
therefore he will rise up to show you
compassion.
For the LORD is a God of justice.
Blessed are all who wait for him!

ISAIAH 30:18

As a father has compassion on his children,
so the LORD has compassion on those who
fear him.

PSALM 103:13

I will betroth you to me forever;
I will betroth you in righteousness
and justice,
in love and compassion.

HOSEA 2:19

COMPASSION

"Though the mountains be shaken
and the hills be removed,
yet my unfailing love for you will not be shaken
nor my covenant of peace be removed,"
says the LORD, who has compassion on you.

ISAIAH 54:10

Your compassion, LORD, is great;
preserve my life according to your laws.

PSALM 119:156

Because of the LORD's great love we are not
consumed,
for his compassions never fail.
They are new every morning;
great is your faithfulness.

LAMENTATIONS 3:22-23

CONFIDENCE

The LORD will be at your side
and will keep your foot from being snared.

PROVERBS 3:26

We say with confidence,
"The Lord is my helper; I will not be afraid.
What can mere mortals do to me?"

HEBREWS 13:6

Though an army besiege me,
my heart will not fear;
though war break out against me,
even then will I be confident.

PSALM 27:3

Even though I walk
through the darkest valley,
I will fear no evil,
for you are with me;
your rod and your staff,
they comfort me.

PSALM 23:4

CONFIDENCE

We know and rely on the love God has for us. God is love. Whoever lives in love lives in God, and God in them. This is how love is made complete among us so that we will have confidence on the day of judgment: In this world we are like Jesus.

1 JOHN 4:16-17

Such confidence we have through Christ before God. Not that we are competent in ourselves to claim anything for ourselves, but our competence comes from God.

2 CORINTHIANS 3:4-5

Let us then approach God's throne of grace with confidence, so that we may receive mercy and find grace to help us in our time of need.

HEBREWS 4:16

This is the confidence we have in approaching God: that if we ask anything according to his will, he hears us.

1 JOHN 5:14

CONTENTMENT

I have learned to be content whatever the circumstances. I know what it is to be in need, and I know what it is to have plenty. I have learned the secret of being content in any and every situation, whether well fed or hungry, whether living in plenty or in want. I can do all this through him who gives me strength.

PHILIPPIANS 4:11-13

The fear of the LORD leads to life:
    Then one rests content, untouched
        by trouble.

PROVERBS 19:23

Godliness with contentment is great gain.

1 TIMOTHY 6:6

Keep your lives free from the love of money and be content with what you have, because God has said,

"Never will I leave you;
    never will I forsake you."

HEBREWS 13:5

CONTENTMENT

Naked I came from my mother's womb,
and naked I will depart.
The LORD gave and the LORD has taken away;
may the name of the LORD be praised.

JOB 1:21

If we have food and clothing, we will be
content with that.

1 TIMOTHY 6:8

The cheerful heart has a continual feast.

PROVERBS 15:15

John answered, "Anyone who has two shirts
should share with the one who has none, and
anyone who has food should do the same."
Even tax collectors came to be baptized.
"Teacher," they asked, "what should we do?"
"Don't collect any more than you are required
to," he told them. Then some soldiers asked
him, "And what should we do?"

LUKE 3:11-14

COURAGE

Be strong and take heart,
all you who hope in the LORD.

PSALM 31:24

When I am afraid, I put my trust in you.
In God, whose word I praise—
in God I trust and am not afraid.

PSALM 56:3-4

"When you pass through the waters,
I will be with you;
and when you pass through the rivers,
they will not sweep over you.
When you walk through the fire,
you will not be burned;
the flames will not set you ablaze.
For I am the LORD your God,
the Holy One of Israel, your Savior."

ISAIAH 43:2-3

The LORD your God, who is among you, is a
great and awesome God.

DEUTERONOMY 7:21

COURAGE

Have no fear of sudden disaster
    or of the ruin that overtakes the wicked,
for the LORD will be at your side and will
    keep your foot from being snared.

PROVERBS 3:25-26

"I will strengthen you and help you;
    I will uphold you with my righteous
        right hand."

ISAIAH 41:10

The LORD is my light and my salvation —
    whom shall I fear?
The LORD is the stronghold of my life —
    of whom shall I be afraid?

PSALM 27:1

"Be strong and courageous. Do not be afraid or
terrified because of them, for the LORD your
God goes with you; he will never leave you nor
forsake you."

DEUTERONOMY 31:6

With your help I can advance against a troop;
    with my God I can scale a wall.

PSALM 18:29

DECISIONS

This is what the LORD says:

"Stand at the crossroads and look;
ask for the ancient paths,
ask where the good way is, and walk in it,
and you will find rest for your souls."

JEREMIAH 6:16

If any of you lacks wisdom, you should ask God, who gives generously to all without finding fault, and it will be given to you.

JAMES 1:5

"Call to me and I will answer you and tell you great and unsearchable things you do not know."

JEREMIAH 33:3

"I will ask the Father, and he will give you another advocate to help you and be with you forever—the Spirit of truth. The world cannot accept him, because it neither sees him nor knows him. But you know him, for he lives with you and will be in you."

JOHN 14:16-17

DECISIONS

This is what the LORD Almighty says: "Give careful thought to your ways."

HAGGAI 1:5

Trust in the LORD with all your heart
and lean not on your own understanding;
in all your ways submit to him,
and he will make your paths straight.

PROVERBS 3:5-6

In their hearts humans plan their course,
but the LORD establishes their steps.

PROVERBS 16:9

Commit your way to the LORD;
trust in him.

PSALM 37:5

Take delight in the LORD
and he will give you the desires of
your heart.

PSALM 37:4

DISCERNMENT

"When he, the Spirit of truth, comes, he will guide you into all the truth. He will not speak on his own; he will speak only what he hears, and he will tell you what is yet to come."

JOHN 16:13

We are from God, and whoever knows God listens to us; but whoever is not from God does not listen to us. This is how we recognize the Spirit of truth and the spirit of falsehood.

1 JOHN 4:6

Test the spirits to see whether they are from God, because many false prophets have gone out into the world.

1 JOHN 4:1

Test them all; hold on to what is good, reject every kind of evil.

1 THESSALONIANS 5:21-22

We know that we have come to know him if we keep his commands.

1 JOHN 2:3

DISCERNMENT

The person without the Spirit does not accept the things that come from the Spirit of God but considers them foolishness, and cannot understand them because they are discerned only through the Spirit. The person with the Spirit makes judgments about all things, but such a person is not subject to merely human judgments, for, "Who has known the mind of the Lord so as to instruct him?" But we have the mind of Christ.

1 Corinthians 2:14-16

Do not believe every spirit, but test the spirits to see whether they are from God…. This is how you can recognize the Spirit of God: Every spirit that acknowledges that Jesus Christ has come in the flesh is from God.

1 John 4:1-2

DISCIPLESHIP

"Whoever serves me must follow me; and where I am, my servant also will be. My Father will honor the one who serves me."

JOHN 12:26

Jesus said to his disciples, "Whoever wants to be my disciple must deny themselves and take up their cross and follow me. For whoever wants to save their life will lose it, but whoever loses their life for me will find it."

MATTHEW 16:24-25

When Jesus spoke again to the people, he said, "I am the light of the world. Whoever follows me will never walk in darkness, but will have the light of life."

JOHN 8:12

If they obey and serve him,
they will spend the rest of their days
in prosperity
and their years in contentment.

JOB 36:11

DISCIPLESHIP

"Whoever has my commands and keeps them is the one who loves me. The one who loves me will be loved by my Father, and I too will love them and show myself to them."

John 14:21

"This is to my Father's glory, that you bear much fruit, showing yourselves to be my disciples."

John 15:8

"Everyone will know that you are my disciples, if you love one another."

John 13:35

In the presence of God and of Christ Jesus, who will judge the living and the dead, and in view of his appearing and his kingdom, I give you this charge: Preach the Word; be prepared in season and out of season; correct, rebuke and encourage — with great patience and careful instruction.

2 Timothy 4:1-2

ENCOURAGEMENT

May our Lord Jesus Christ himself and God our Father, who loved us and by his grace gave us eternal encouragement and good hope, encourage your hearts and strengthen you in every good deed and word.

2 THESSALONIANS 2:16-17

You, LORD, hear the desire of the afflicted;
*   you encourage them, and you listen to*
*   their cry.*

PSALM 10:17

The LORD is good to those whose hope is
*   in him,*
*   to the one who seeks him;*
it is good to wait quietly
*   for the salvation of the LORD.*

LAMENTATIONS 3:25-26

"I know the plans I have for you," declares the LORD, "plans to prosper you and not to harm you, plans to give you hope and a future."

JEREMIAH 29:11

ENCOURAGEMENT

This I call to mind
and therefore I have hope:
*Because of the L*ORD*'s great love we are*
not consumed,
for his compassions never fail.
They are new every morning;
great is your faithfulness.

LAMENTATIONS 3:21-23

*The L*ORD *will not reject his people;*
he will never forsake his inheritance.
Judgment will again be founded on
righteousness,
and all the upright in heart will follow it.

PSALM 94:14-15

*Cast your cares on the L*ORD
and he will sustain you;
he will never let the righteous be shaken.

PSALM 55:22

Encourage one another and build each other
up, just as in fact you are doing.

1 THESSALONIANS 5:11

ETERNAL LIFE

The world and its desires pass away, but whoever who does the will of God lives forever.

1 John 2:17

The wages of sin is death, but the gift of God is eternal life in Christ Jesus our Lord.

Romans 6:23

"God so loved the world that he gave his one and only Son, that whoever believes in him shall not perish but have eternal life."

John 3:16

This is the testimony: God has given us eternal life, and this life is in his Son. Whoever has the Son has life; whoever does not have the Son of God does not have life.

1 John 5:11-12

ETERNAL LIFE

"Whoever believes in the Son has eternal life."

JOHN 3:36

Having been justified by his grace, we might become heirs having the hope of eternal life.

TITUS 3:7

"My sheep listen to my voice; I know them, and they follow me. I give them eternal life, and they shall never perish; no one will snatch them out of my hand. My Father, who has given them to me, is greater than all; no one can snatch them out of my Father's hand."

JOHN 10:27-29

"This is eternal life: that they know you, the only true God, and Jesus Christ, whom you have sent."

JOHN 17:3

FAITH

Faith is confidence in what we hope for and
assurance about what we do not see.

HEBREWS 11:1

Through [Christ] you believe in God, who
raised him from the dead and glorified him,
and so your faith and hope are in God.

1 PETER 1:21

Though you have not seen [Christ], you love
him; and even though you do not see him now,
you believe in him and are filled with an
inexpressible and glorious joy.

1 PETER 1:8

This is a trustworthy saying that deserves full
acceptance. That is why we labor and strive,
because we have put our hope in the living
God, who is the Savior of all people, and
especially of those who believe.

1 TIMOTHY 4:9-10

May your unfailing love be with us, Lord,
even as we put our hope in you.

PSALM 33:22

FAITH

Since we have been justified through faith, we have peace with God through our Lord Jesus Christ.

ROMANS 5:1

"Very truly I tell you, whoever believes in me will do the works I have been doing, and they will do even greater things than these, because I am going to the Father."

JOHN 14:12

"Truly I tell you, if you have faith as small as a mustard seed, you can say to this mountain, 'Move from here to there' and it will move. Nothing will be impossible for you."

MATTHEW 17:20

Those who hope in the LORD
will renew their strength.
They will soar on wings like eagles;
they will run and not grow weary,
they will walk and not be faint.

ISAIAH 40:31

FAITHFULNESS

Let love and faithfulness never leave you;
*   bind them around your neck,*
*   write them on the tablet of your heart.*
Then you will win favor and a good name
*   in the sight of God and man.*

PROVERBS 3:3-4

Love the LORD, all his faithful people!
*   The LORD preserves those who are true*
*   to him,*
but the proud he pays back in full.

PSALM 31:23

To the faithful you show yourself faithful,
*   to the blameless you show yourself*
*   blameless.*

2 SAMUEL 22:26

The LORD loves the just
*   and will not forsake his faithful ones.*

PSALM 37:28

FAITHFULNESS

He holds success in store for the upright,
*   he is a shield to those whose walk*
*   is blameless,*
for he guards the course of the just
*   and protects the way of his faithful ones.*

PROVERBS 2:7–8

Do not those who plot evil go astray?
*   But those who plan what is good find love*
*   and faithfulness.*

PROVERBS 14:22

"Be faithful, even to the point of death, and I
will give you life as your victor's crown."

REVELATION 2:10

If anyone is to go into captivity,
*   into captivity they will go.*
If anyone is to be killed with the sword,
*   with the sword they will be killed.*
This calls for patient endurance and faithful-
*   ness on the part of God's people.*

REVELATION 13:10

FAITHFULNESS OF GOD

God is faithful, who has called you into
fellowship with his Son, Jesus Christ our Lord.

1 CORINTHIANS 1:9

The LORD is good and his love endures forever;
  his faithfulness continues through all
    generations.

PSALM 100:5

"Though the mountains be shaken
  and the hills be removed,
yet my unfailing love for you will not be shaken
  nor my covenant of peace be removed,"
says the LORD, who has compassion on you.

ISAIAH 54:10

Because of the LORD's great love we are
      not consumed,
    for his compassions never fail.
They are new every morning;
  great is your faithfulness.

LAMENTATIONS 3:22-23

FAITHFULNESS OF GOD

The works of his hands are faithful and just;
*   all his precepts are trustworthy.*
They are established for ever and ever,
*   enacted in faithfulness and uprightness.*

PSALM 111:7-8

Know therefore that the LORD your God is God;
he is the faithful God, keeping his covenant of
love to a thousand generations of those who
love him and keep his commandments.

DEUTERONOMY 7:9

If we confess our sins, he is faithful and just
and will forgive us our sins and purify us from
all unrighteousness.

1 JOHN 1:9

Great is your love, higher than the heavens;
*   your faithfulness reaches to the skies.*

PSALM 108:4

The Lord is faithful, and he will strengthen
you and protect you from the evil one.

2 THESSALONIANS 3:3

FINANCES

[Jesus] said to them, "Watch out! Be on your guard against all kinds of greed; life does not consist in the abundance of possessions."

LUKE 12:15

Keep your lives free from the love of money and be content with what you have, because God has said,

"Never will I leave you;
never will I forsake you."

HEBREWS 13:5

"Whoever can be trusted with very little can also be trusted with much, and whoever is dishonest with very little will also be dishonest with much."

LUKE 16:10

Honor the LORD with your wealth,
with the firstfruits of all your crops;
then your barns will be filled to overflowing,
and your vats will brim over with new wine.

PROVERBS 3:9-10

FINANCES

"Bring the whole tithe into the storehouse, that there may be food in my house. Test me in this," says the LORD Almighty, "and see if I will not throw open the floodgates of heaven and pour out so much blessing that there will not be room enough to store it."

MALACHI 3:10

My God will meet all your needs according to the glorious riches in Christ Jesus.

PHILIPPIANS 4:19

Whoever gathers money little by little makes it grow.

PROVERBS 13:11

Let no debt remain outstanding, except the continuing debt to love one another, for whoever loves others has fulfilled the law.

ROMANS 13:8

*A good person leaves an inheritance for their children's children,
but a sinner's wealth is stored up for the righteous.*

PROVERBS 13:22

FORGIVENESS OF GOD

Peter replied, "Repent and be baptized, every one of you, in the name of Jesus Christ for the forgiveness of your sins. And you will receive the gift of the Holy Spirit."

ACTS 2:38

There is now no condemnation for those who are in Christ Jesus, because through Christ Jesus the law of the Spirit who gives life has set you free from the law of sin and death.

ROMANS 8:1-2

In [Jesus] we have redemption through his blood, the forgiveness of sins, in accordance with the riches of God's grace.

EPHESIANS 1:7

When you were dead in your sins and in the uncircumcision of your flesh, God made you alive with Christ. He forgave us all our sins, having canceled the charge of our legal indebtedness, which stood against us and condemned us; he has taken it away, nailing it to the cross.

COLOSSIANS 2:13-14

FORGIVENESS OF GOD

You are a forgiving God, gracious and compassionate, slow to anger and abounding in love.

NEHEMIAH 9:17

If we confess our sins, he is faithful and just and will forgive us our sins and purify us from all unrighteousness.

1 JOHN 1:9

"If you forgive other people when they sin against you, your heavenly Father will also forgive you."

MATTHEW 6:14

As far as the east is from the west,
so far has he removed our transgressions
from us.

PSALM 103:12

I acknowledged my sin to you
and did not cover up my iniquity.
I said, "I will confess
my transgressions to the LORD."
And you forgave
the guilt of my sin.

PSALM 32:5

FREEDOM

The Spirit of the Sovereign LORD *is on me,*
  because the LORD *has anointed me*
  to proclaim good news to the poor.
He has sent me to bind up the brokenhearted,
  to proclaim freedom for the captives
  and release from darkness for the prisoners.
ISAIAH 61:1

Anyone who has died has been set free from sin.
ROMANS 6:7

Jesus said, "If you hold to my teaching, you are really my disciples. Then you will know the truth, and the truth will set you free."
JOHN 8:31-32

The creation itself will be liberated from its bondage to decay and brought into the freedom and glory of the children of God.
ROMANS 8:21

"If the Son sets you free, you will be free indeed."
JOHN 8:36

FREEDOM

The Lord is the Spirit, and where the Spirit of the Lord is, there is freedom.

2 CORINTHIANS 3:17

Through Christ Jesus the law of the Spirit who gives life has set you free from the law of sin and death.

ROMANS 8:2

Now that you have been set free from sin and have become slaves to God, the benefit you reap leads to holiness, and the result is eternal life.

ROMANS 6:22

It is for freedom that Christ has set us free. Stand firm, then, and do not let yourselves be burdened again by a yoke of slavery.

GALATIANS 5:1

By dying to what once bound us, we have been released from the law so that we serve in the new way of the Spirit, and not in the old way of the written code.

ROMANS 7:6

FRIENDSHIP

A friend loves at all times,
and a brother is born for a time of adversity.

PROVERBS 17:17

Be devoted to one another in love. Honor one another above yourselves.

ROMANS 12:10

"Greater love has no one than this, to lay down one's life for one's friends."

JOHN 15:13

Two are better than one,
because they have a good return for their
labor:
If either of them falls down,
one can help the other up.
But pity anyone who falls
and has no one to help them up.

ECCLESIASTES 4:9-10

FRIENDSHIP

One who has unreliable friends soon comes
    to ruin,
    but there is a friend who sticks closer than a
    brother.

PROVERBS 18:24

Walk with the wise and become wise,
    for a companion of fools suffers harm.

PROVERBS 13:20

As iron sharpens iron,
    so one person sharpens another.

PROVERBS 27:17

Wounds from a friend can be trusted,
    but an enemy multiplies kisses.

PROVERBS 27:6

How good and pleasant it is
    when God's people live together in unity!

PSALM 133:1

FUTURE

As it is written:

"What no eye has seen,
*   what no ear has heard,*
and what no human mind has conceived"—
*   the things God has prepared for those who*
*   love him—*

these are the things God has revealed to us by his Spirit.

1 Corinthians 2:9-10

Our citizenship is in heaven. And we eagerly await a Savior from there, the Lord Jesus Christ, who, by the power that enables him to bring everything under his control, will transform our lowly bodies so that they will be like his glorious body.

Philippians 3:20-21

Listen, I tell you a mystery: We will not all sleep, but we will all be changed—in a flash, in the twinkling of an eye, at the last trumpet. For the trumpet will sound, the dead will be raised imperishable, and we will be changed.

1 Corinthians 15:51-52

FUTURE

We are children of God, and what we will be has not yet been made known. But we know that when Christ appears, we shall be like him, for we shall see him as he is.

1 JOHN 3:2

"I know the plans I have for you," declares the LORD, "plans to prosper you and not to harm you, plans to give you hope and a future."

JEREMIAH 29:11

The plans of the LORD stand firm forever,
*   the purposes of his heart through all*
*   generations.*

PSALM 33:11

Why, you do not even know what will happen tomorrow. What is your life? You are a mist that appears for a little while and then vanishes. Instead, you ought to say, "If it is the Lord's will, we will live and do this or that."

JAMES 4:14-15

GIVING

Each of you should give what you have decided in your heart to give, not reluctantly or under compulsion, for God loves a cheerful giver.

2 Corinthians 9:7

"Give, and it will be given to you. A good measure, pressed down, shaken together and running over, will be poured into your lap. For with the measure you use, it will be measured to you."

Luke 6:38

*Good will come to those who are generous and
    lend freely,
  who conduct their affairs with justice.*

Psalm 112:5

*A generous person will prosper;
  whoever refreshes others will be refreshed.*

Proverbs 11:25

GIVING

The generous will themselves be blessed,
for they share their food with the poor.

PROVERBS 22:9

"When you give to the needy, do not let your
left hand know what your right hand is doing,
so that your giving may be in secret. Then your
Father, who sees what is done in secret, will
reward you."

MATTHEW 6:3-4

If your enemy is hungry, give him food to eat;
if he is thirsty, give him water to drink.

PROVERBS 25:21

Those who give to the poor will lack nothing,
but those who close their eyes to them
receive many curses.

PROVERBS 28:27

GOALS

We make it our goal to please him, whether we are at home in the body or away from it.

2 CORINTHIANS 5:9

"Seek first his kingdom and his righteousness, and all these things will be given to you as well."

MATTHEW 6:33

Do you not know that in a race all the runners run, but only one gets the prize? Run in such a way as to get the prize.

1 CORINTHIANS 9:24

Brothers and sisters, I do not consider myself yet to have taken hold of it. But one thing I do: Forgetting what is behind and straining toward what is ahead, I press on toward the goal to win the prize for which God has called me heavenward in Christ Jesus.

PHILIPPIANS 3:13-14

Do your best to present yourself to God as one approved, a workman who does not need to be ashamed and who correctly handles the word of truth.

2 TIMOTHY 2:15

GOALS

As God's chosen people, holy and dearly loved, clothe yourselves with compassion, kindness, humility, gentleness and patience.

COLOSSIANS 3:12

In your hearts revere Christ as Lord. Always be prepared to give an answer to everyone who asks you to give the reason for the hope that you have. But do this with gentleness and respect.

1 PETER 3:15

Since you are eager for gifts of the Spirit, try to excel in those that build up the church.

1 CORINTHIANS 14:12

Make it your ambition to lead a quiet life: You should mind your own business and work with your hands, just as we told you.

1 THESSALONIANS 4:11

GOODNESS OF GOD

The LORD is good to all;
*   he has compassion on all he has made.*

PSALM 145:9

Good and upright is the LORD;
*   therefore he instructs sinners in his ways.*

PSALM 25:8

The LORD is good,
*   a refuge in times of trouble.*
He cares for those who trust in him.

NAHUM 1:7

How abundant are the good things
*   that you have stored up for those who*
*   fear you,*
that you bestow in the sight of all,
*   on those who take refuge in you.*

PSALM 31:19

The LORD is good to those whose hope is in him,
*   to the one who seeks him.*

LAMENTATIONS 3:25

GOODNESS OF GOD

I remain confident of this:
   I will see the goodness of the LORD
   in the land of the living.

PSALM 27:13

[God's] divine power has given us everything
we need for a godly life through our
knowledge of him who called us by his own
glory and goodness.

2 PETER 1:3

I say to the LORD, "You are my LORD;
   apart from you I have no good thing."

PSALM 16:2

We know that in all things God works for the
good of those who love him, who have been
called according to his purpose.

ROMANS 8:28

GRACE

God raised us up with Christ and seated us with him in the heavenly realms in Christ Jesus, in order that in the coming ages he might show the incomparable riches of his grace, expressed in his kindness to us in Christ Jesus.

EPHESIANS 2:6-7

It is by grace you have been saved, through faith—and this not from yourselves, it is the gift of God—not by works, so that no one can boast.

EPHESIANS 2:8-9

You know the grace of our Lord Jesus Christ, that though he was rich, yet for your sake he became poor, so that you through his poverty might become rich.

2 CORINTHIANS 8:9

GRACE

Out of his fullness we have all received grace
in place of grace already given.

JOHN 1:16

God is able to bless you abundantly, so that in
all things at all times, having all that you need,
you will abound in every good work.

2 CORINTHIANS 9:8

[God] saved us, not because of righteous
things we had done, but because of his mercy.
He saved us through the washing of rebirth
and renewal by the Holy Spirit, whom he
poured out on us generously through Jesus
Christ our Savior, so that, having been justified
by his grace, we might become heirs having the
hope of eternal life.

TITUS 3:5-7

GUIDANCE

In your unfailing love you will lead
*   the people you have redeemed.*
In your strength you will guide them
*   to your holy dwelling.*

Exodus 15:13

[The Lord] makes me lie down in green pastures,
*   he leads me beside quiet waters,*
*   he refreshes my soul.*
He guides me along the right paths
*   for his name's sake.*

Psalm 23:2-3

The Lord will guide you always;
*   he will satisfy your needs in a sun-*
*   scorched land*
*   and will strengthen your frame.*
You will be like a well-watered garden,
*   like a spring whose waters never fail.*

Isaiah 58:11

GUIDANCE

If I rise on the wings of the dawn,
   if I settle on the far side of the sea,
even there your hand will guide me,
   your right hand will hold me fast.

PSALM 139:9-10

The LORD makes firm the steps
   of the one who delights in him;
though he may stumble, he will not fall,
   for the LORD upholds him with his hand.

PSALM 37:23-24

"I will lead the blind by ways they have
     not known,
   along unfamiliar paths I will guide them;
I will turn the darkness into light before them
   and make the rough places smooth.
These are the things I will do;
   I will not forsake them."

ISAIAH 42:16

HEALING

"I will heal my people and will let them enjoy abundant peace and security."

JEREMIAH 33:6

"I will heal their waywardness
and love them freely,
for my anger has turned away from them."

HOSEA 14:4

He himself bore our sins in his body on the tree, so that we might die to sins and live for righteousness; by his wounds you have been healed.

1 PETER 2:24

Praise the LORD, my soul,
and forget not all his benefits—
who forgives all your sins
and heals all your diseases.

PSALM 103:2-3

HEALING

"I will restore you to health
    and heal your wounds,"
declares the LORD,
    "because you are called an outcast,
Zion for whom no one cares."

JEREMIAH 30:17

Heal me, LORD, and I will be healed;
    save me and I will be saved,
    for you are the one I praise.

JEREMIAH 17:14

The prayer offered in faith will make the sick
person well; the Lord will raise them up. If
they have has sinned, they will be forgiven.
Therefore confess your sins to each other and
pray for each other so that you may be healed.
The prayer of a righteous person is powerful
and effective.

JAMES 5:15-16

LORD my God, I called to you for help
    and you healed me.

PSALM 30:2

HEAVEN

"My Father's house has many rooms; if that were not so, would I have told you that I am going there to prepare a place for you? And if I go and prepare a place for you, I will come back and take you to be with me that you also may be where I am."

JOHN 14:2-3

[God] will wipe every tear from their eyes. There will be no more death or mourning or crying or pain, for the old order of things has passed away.

REVELATION 21:4

Never again will they hunger;
*   never again will they thirst.*
The sun will not beat upon them,
*   nor any scorching heat.*
For the Lamb at the center of the throne will be
*   their shepherd;*
*   he will lead them to springs of living water.*
And God will wipe away every tear from
*   their eyes.*

REVELATION 7:16-17

HEAVEN

Our citizenship is in heaven. And we
eagerly await a Savior from there, the Lord
Jesus Christ.

PHILIPPIANS 3:20

I heard what sounded like a great multitude,
like the roar of rushing waters and like loud
peals of thunder, shouting:
"Hallelujah!
For our Lord God Almighty reigns."

REVELATION 19:6

According to the Lord's word, we tell you that
we who are still alive, who are left until the
coming of the Lord, will certainly not precede
those who have fallen asleep. For the Lord
himself will come down from heaven, with a
loud command, with the voice of the
archangel and with the trumpet call of God,
and the dead in Christ will rise first. After
that, we who are still alive and are left will be
caught up together with them in the clouds
to meet the Lord in the air. And so we will be
with the Lord forever. Therefore encourage
one another with these words.

1 THESSALONIANS 4:15-18

HOLINESS

May God himself, the God of peace, sanctify you through and through. May your whole spirit, soul and body be kept blameless at the coming of our Lord Jesus Christ.

1 THESSALONIANS 5:23

Just as [God] who called you is holy, so be holy in all you do; for it is written: "Be holy, because I am holy."

1 PETER 1:15-16

God did not call us to be impure, but to live a holy life.

1 THESSALONIANS 4:7

[God] chose us in him before the creation of the world to be holy and blameless in his sight. In love he predestined us for adoption to sonship through Jesus Christ, in accordance with his pleasure and will—to the praise of his glorious grace, which he has freely given us in the One he loves.

EPHESIANS 1:4-6

HOLINESS

Since we have these promises, dear friends, let us purify ourselves from everything that contaminates body and spirit, perfecting holiness out of reverence for God.

2 CORINTHIANS 7:1

Now that you have been set free from sin and have become slaves of God, the benefit you reap leads to holiness, and the result is eternal life.

ROMANS 6:22

Make every effort to live in peace with everyone and to be holy; without holiness no one will see the Lord.

HEBREWS 12:14

Blessed are they whose ways are blameless,
who walk according to the law of the LORD.
PSALM 119:1

The righteousness of the blameless makes their
paths straight,
but the wicked are brought down by their
own wickedness.
PROVERBS 11:5

HONESTY

You desired faithfulness even in the womb;
*   you taught me wisdom in that secret place.*

PSALM 51:6

Love … rejoices with the truth.

1 CORINTHIANS 13:6

Stand firm then, with the belt of truth buckled
around your waist, with the breastplate of
righteousness in place.

EPHESIANS 6:14

Whoever of you loves life
*   and desires to see many good days,*
keep your tongue from evil
*   and your lips from telling lies.*

PSALM 34:12-13

Whoever walks in integrity walks securely,
*   but whoever takes crooked paths will be*
*   found out.*

PROVERBS 10:9

HONESTY

The righteous hate what is false.

PROVERBS 13:5

The one whose walk is blameless
    and who does what is righteous,
who speaks the truth from their heart ...
Whoever does these things
    will never be shaken.

PSALM 15:2, 5

"Those who walk righteously
    and speak what is right ...
they are the ones who will dwell on the heights,
    whose refuge will be the mountain fortress.
Their bread will be supplied,
    and water will not fail them."

ISAIAH 33:15-16

An honest answer
    is like a kiss on the lips.

PROVERBS 24:26

HOPE

This is a trustworthy saying that deserves full acceptance. That is why we labor and strive, because we have put our hope in the living God, who is the Savior of all people, and especially of those who believe.

1 TIMOTHY 4:9-10

My heart is glad and my tongue rejoices;
my body also will rest in hope,
because you will not abandon me of the dead,
you will not let your Holy One see decay.

ACTS 2:26-27

This I call to mind
and therefore I have hope:
Because of the LORD's great love
we are not consumed,
for his compassions never fail.

LAMENTATIONS 3:21-22

The LORD delights in those who fear him,
who put their hope in his unfailing love.

PSALM 147:11

HOPE

*Those who hope in the L*ORD
will renew their strength.
They will soar on wings like eagles;
they will run and not grow weary,
they will walk and not be faint.

ISAIAH 40:31

Why, my soul, are you downcast?
Why so disturbed within me?
Put your hope in God,
for I will yet praise him,
my Savior and my God.

PSALM 42:5-6

May the God of hope fill you with all joy
and peace as you trust in him, so that you
may overflow with hope by the power of the
Holy Spirit.

ROMANS 15:13

HUMILITY

*Humility is the fear of the L*ORD*,*
    its wages are riches and honor and life.

PROVERBS 22:4

Humble yourselves before the Lord, and he
will lift you up.

JAMES 4:10

*The L*ORD *takes delight in his people;*
    he crowns the humble with victory.

PSALM 149:4

*Wisdom's instruction is to fear the L*ORD*,*
    and humility comes before honor.

PROVERBS 15:33

*The L*ORD *sustains the humble*
    but casts the wicked to the ground.

PSALM 147:6

*[The L*ORD*] guides the humble in what is right*
    and teaches them his way.

PSALM 25:9

HUMILITY

"The greatest among you will be your servant.
For those who exalt themselves will be
humbled, and those who humble themselves
will be exalted."

MATTHEW 23:11-12

"Whoever takes the lowly position of this child
is the greatest in the kingdom of heaven."

MATTHEW 18:4

Do nothing out of selfish ambition or vain
conceit. Rather, in humility value others above
yourselves.

PHILIPPIANS 2:3

Remind the people to be subject to rulers
and authorities, to be obedient, to be ready to
do whatever is good, to slander no one, to be
peaceable and considerate, and always to be
gentle toward everyone.

TITUS 3:1-2

IDENTITY

*Now, this is what the L*ORD* says —*
  he who created you, Jacob,
  he who formed you, Israel:
  "Do not fear, for I have redeemed you;
I have summoned you by name; you are mine."

ISAIAH 43:1

*Know that the L*ORD* is God.*
  It is he who made us, and we are his;
we are his people, the sheep of his pasture.

PSALM 100:3

For the sake of his great name the LORD will
not reject his people, because the LORD was
pleased to make you his own.

1 SAMUEL 12:22

You are a chosen people, a royal priesthood, a
holy nation, God's special possession, that you
may declare the praises of him who called you
out of darkness into his wonderful light.

1 PETER 2:9

IDENTITY

Come, let us bow down in worship,
*let us kneel before the L*ORD *our Maker;*
for he is our God
and we are the people of his pasture,
the flock under his care.

PSALM 95:6-7

You also were included in Christ when you heard the message of truth, the gospel of your salvation. When you believed, you were marked in him with a seal, the promised Holy Spirit.

EPHESIANS 1:13

We are God's handiwork, created in Christ Jesus to do good works, which God prepared in advance for us to do.

EPHESIANS 2:10

As God's chosen people, holy and dearly loved, clothe yourselves with compassion, kindness, humility, gentleness and patience.

COLOSSIANS 3:12

INTEGRITY

I know, my God, that you test the heart and are pleased with integrity.

1 Chronicles 29:17

The LORD God is a sun and shield;
    the LORD bestows favor and honor;
no good thing does he withhold
    from those whose walk is blameless.

Psalm 84:11

[God] holds success in store for the upright,
    he is a shield to those whose walk
        is blameless,
for he guards the course of the just
    and protects the way of his faithful ones.

Proverbs 2:7–8

Whoever walks in integrity walks securely,
    but whoever takes crooked paths will be
        found out.

Proverbs 10:9

INTEGRITY

*The integrity of the upright guides them,
    but the unfaithful are destroyed by their
    duplicity.*

PROVERBS 11:3

*Because of my integrity you uphold me
    and set me in your presence forever.*

PSALM 41:12

*Those who walk uprightly
    enter into peace;
    they find rest as they lie in death.*

ISAIAH 57:2

*When the LORD takes pleasure in anyone's way,
    he causes their enemies to make peace
        with them.*

PROVERBS 16:7

Someone will say, "You have faith; I have
deeds." Show me your faith without deeds, and
I will show you my faith by my deeds.

JAMES 2:18

JOY

You have loved righteousness and hated
    wickedness;
therefore God, your God, has set you above
    your companions
by anointing you with the oil of joy.

HEBREWS 1:9

[God] will yet fill your mouth with laughter
    and your lips with shouts of joy.

JOB 8:21

You make me glad by your deeds, LORD;
    I sing for joy at what your hands have done.

PSALM 92:4

Though you have not seen him, you love him;
and even though you do not see him now,
you believe in him and are filled with an
inexpressible and glorious joy, for you are
receiving the end result of your faith, the
salvation of your souls.

1 PETER 1:8-9

JOY

Consider it pure joy, my brothers and sisters, whenever you face trials of many kinds, because you know that the testing of your faith produces perseverance.

JAMES 1:2-3

"Until now you have not asked for anything in my name. Ask and you will receive, and your joy will be complete."

JOHN 16:24

Therefore my heart is glad and my
*   tongue rejoices;*
*   my body also will rest in hope,*
because you will not abandon me to the realm
*   of the dead,*
*   you will not let your holy one see decay.*
You have made known to me the paths of life;
*   you will fill me with joy in your presence.*

ACTS 2:26-28

LIFE

Jesus declared, "I am the bread of life. Whoever comes to me will never go hungry, and whoever believes in me will never be thirsty."

JOHN 6:35

Set your hearts on things above, where Christ is seated, at the right hand of God. Set your minds on things above, not on earthly things. For you died, and your life is now hidden with Christ in God. When Christ, who is your life, appears, then you also will appear with him in glory.

COLOSSIANS 3:1-4

Count yourselves dead to sin but alive to God in Christ Jesus.

ROMANS 6:11

Through Christ Jesus the law of the Spirit who gives life has set you free from the law of sin and death.

ROMANS 8:2

"The Spirit gives life; the flesh counts for nothing. The words I have spoken to you— they are full of the Spirit and life."

JOHN 6:63

LIFE

If the Spirit of him who raised Jesus from the dead is living in you, he who raised Christ from the dead will also give life to your mortal bodies because of his Spirit who lives in you.

ROMANS 8:11

The Spirit of God has made me;
  the breath of the Almighty gives me life.

JOB 33:4

You have made known to me the paths of life;
  you will fill me with joy in your presence.

ACTS 2:28

My son, do not forget my teaching,
  but keep my commands in your heart,
for they will prolong your life many years
  and bring you peace and prosperity.

PROVERBS 3:1-2

LOVE FOR OTHERS

If you really keep the royal law found in Scripture, "Love your neighbor as yourself," you are doing right.

JAMES 2:8

We love because he first loved us.

1 JOHN 4:19

Dear friends, let us love one another, for love comes from God. Everyone who loves has been born of God and knows God.

1 JOHN 4:7

As God's chosen people, holy and dearly loved, clothe yourselves with compassion, kindness, humility, gentleness and patience. Bear with each other and forgive one another if any of you has a grievance against someone. Forgive as the Lord forgave you. And over all these virtues put on love, which binds them all together in perfect unity.

COLOSSIANS 3:12-14

No one has ever seen God; but if we love one another, God lives in us and his love is made complete in us.

1 JOHN 4:12

LOVE FOR OTHERS

Love each other deeply, because love covers over a multitude of sins.

1 PETER 4:8

In humility value others above yourselves, not looking to your own interests but each of you to the interests of the others.

PHILIPPIANS 2:3-4

Anyone who loves their brother and sister lives in the light, and there is nothing in them to make them stumble.

1 JOHN 2:10

"I tell you: love your enemies and pray for those who persecute you, that you may be children of your Father in heaven."

MATTHEW 5:44-45

Whoever would foster love covers over an offense,
    but whoever repeats the matter separates close friends.

PROVERBS 17:9

LOVE OF GOD

The LORD is gracious and compassionate,
slow to anger and rich in love.

PSALM 145:8

This is love: not that we loved God, but that
he loved us and sent his Son as an atoning
sacrifice for our sins.

1 JOHN 4:10

The LORD appeared to us in the past, saying:
"I have loved you with an everlasting love;
I have drawn you with unfailing kindness."

JEREMIAH 31:3

As a bridegroom rejoices over his bride,
so will your God rejoice over you.

ISAIAH 62:5

From everlasting to everlasting
the LORD's love is with those who fear him,
and his righteousness with their children's
children.

PSALM 103:17

LOVE OF GOD

"I will betroth you to me forever;
I will betroth you in righteousness
and justice,
in love and compassion.
I will betroth you in faithfulness,
and you will acknowledge the LORD."

HOSEA 2:19-20

Because of his great love for us, God, who is rich in mercy, made us alive with Christ even when we were dead in transgressions—it is by grace you have been saved.

EPHESIANS 2:4-5

"The Father himself loves you because you have loved me and have believed that I came from God."

JOHN 16:27

MATURITY

Like newborn babies, crave pure spiritual milk, so that by it you may grow up in your salvation.

1 Peter 2:2

Instruct the wise and they will be wiser still;
teach the righteous and they will add to
their learning.

Proverbs 9:9

Teach us to number our days,
that we may gain a heart of wisdom.

Psalm 90:12

Anyone who lives on milk, being still an infant, is not acquainted with the teaching about righteousness. But solid food is for the mature, who by constant use have trained themselves to distinguish good from evil.

Hebrews 5:13-14

Let us move beyond the elementary teachings about Christ and be taken forward to maturity.

Hebrews 6:1

MATURITY

Perseverance must finish its work so that you may be mature and complete, not lacking anything.

JAMES 1:4

So Christ himself gave the apostles, the prophets, the evangelists, the pastors and teachers, to equip his people for works of service, so that the body of Christ may be built up until we all reach unity in the faith and in the knowledge of the Son of God and become mature, attaining to the whole measure of the fullness of Christ.

EPHESIANS 4:11-13

[God] who began a good work in you will carry it on to completion until the day of Christ Jesus.

PHILIPPIANS 1:6

MEDITATION

Oh, how I love your law!
  I meditate on it all day long.

PSALM 119:97

Blessed is the one
  who does not walk in step with the wicked
or stand in the way that sinners take
  or sit in the company of mockers,
but whose delight is in the law of the LORD,
  and who meditates on his law day and
    night.

PSALM 1:1-2

"Keep this Book of the Law always on your lips; meditate on it day and night, so that you may be careful to do everything written in it. Then you will be prosperous and successful."

JOSHUA 1:8

I will consider all your works
  and meditate on all your mighty deeds.

PSALM 77:12

MEDITATION

I rise before dawn and cry for help;
I have put my hope in your word.
My eyes stay open through the watches of
the night,
that I may meditate on your promises.

PSALM 119:147-148

Within your temple, O God,
we meditate on your unfailing love.

PSALM 48:9

I meditate on your precepts
and consider your ways.

PSALM 119:15

I will sing to the LORD all my life;
I will sing praise to my God as long as I live.
May my meditation be pleasing to him,
as I rejoice in the LORD.

PSALM 104:33-34

May these words of my mouth and this
meditation of my heart
be pleasing in your sight,
LORD, my Rock and my Redeemer.

PSALM 19:14

MERCY OF GOD

The Lord is full of compassion and mercy.

JAMES 5:11

The Lord is gracious and compassionate,
slow to anger and rich in love.

PSALM 145:8

Seek the Lord while he may be found;
call on him while he is near.
Let the wicked forsake their ways
and the unrighteous their thoughts.
Let them turn to the Lord, and he will have
mercy on them,
and to our God, for he will freely pardon.

ISAIAH 55:6-7

Surely it was for my benefit
that I suffered such anguish.
In your love you kept me
from the pit of destruction;
you have put all my sins
behind your back.

ISAIAH 38:17

MERCY OF GOD

The LORD your God is a merciful God; he will not abandon or destroy you or forget the covenant with your ancestors, which he confirmed to them by oath.

DEUTERONOMY 4:31

The LORD has heard my cry for mercy;
the LORD accepts my prayer.

PSALM 6:9

I, by your great love,
can come into your house;
in reverence will I bow down
toward your holy temple.

PSALM 5:7

Who is a God like you,
who pardons sin and forgives the transgression
of the remnant of his inheritance?
You do not stay angry forever
but delight to show mercy.

MICAH 7:18

[God] saved us, not because of righteous things we had done, but because of his mercy. He saved us through the washing of rebirth and renewal by the Holy Spirit.

TITUS 3:5

OBEDIENCE

It is not those who hear the law who are righteous in God's sight, but it is those who obey the law who will be declared righteous.

ROMANS 2:13

[Jesus] replied, "Blessed rather are those who hear the word of God and obey it."

LUKE 11:28

"Everyone who hears these words of mine and puts them into practice is like a wise man who built his house on the rock. The rain came down, the streams rose, and the winds blew and beat against that house; yet it did not fall, because it had its foundation on the rock."

MATTHEW 7:24-25

Whoever looks intently into the perfect law that gives freedom, and continues in it—not forgetting what they have heard, but doing it—they will be blessed in what they do.

JAMES 1:25

"Whoever practices and teaches these commands will be called great in the kingdom of heaven."

MATTHEW 5:19

OBEDIENCE

"If you keep my commands, you will remain in my love, just as I have kept my Father's commands and remain in his love. I have told you this so that my joy may be in you and that your joy may be complete."

JOHN 15:10-11

If anyone obeys his word, love for God is truly made complete in them. This is how we know we are in him.

1 JOHN 2:5

If they obey and serve him,
they will spend the rest of their days
in prosperity
and their years in contentment.

JOB 36:11

I command you today to love the LORD your God, to walk in obedience to him, and to keep his commands, decrees and laws; then you will live and increase, and the LORD your God will bless you in the land you are entering to possess.

DEUTERONOMY 30:16

PARENTS

The righteous lead blameless lives;
*   blessed are their children after them.*

PROVERBS 20:7

Keep his decrees and commands, which I am
giving you today, so that it may go well with
you and your children after you and that you
may live long in the land the LORD your God
gives you for all time.

DEUTERONOMY 4:40

Start children off on the way they should go,
*   and even when they are old they will not*
*   turn from it.*

PROVERBS 22:6

Discipline your children, and they will give
*   you peace;*
*   they will bring you the delights you desire.*

PROVERBS 29:17

A rod and a reprimand impart wisdom,
*   but a child left undisciplined disgraces its*
*   mother.*

PROVERBS 29:15

PARENTS

All your children will be taught by the LORD,
and great will be their peace.

ISAIAH 54:13

These commandments that I give you today
are to be on your hearts. Impress them on
your children. Talk about them when you sit
at home and when you walk along the road,
when you lie down and when you get up.

DEUTERONOMY 6:6-7

Children's children are a crown to the aged,
and parents are the pride of their children.

PROVERBS 17:6

A good person leaves an inheritance for their
children's children,
but a sinner's wealth is stored up for
the righteous.

PROVERBS 13:22

"I have chosen him, so that he will direct his
children and his household after him to keep the
way of the LORD by doing what is right and just."

GENESIS 18:19

PATIENCE

Be joyful in hope, patient in affliction, faithful in prayer.

ROMANS 12:12

Be patient, then, brothers and sisters, until the Lord's coming. See how the farmer waits for the land to yield its valuable crop, patiently waiting for the autumn and spring rains. You too, be patient and stand firm, because the Lord's coming is near.

JAMES 5:7–8

Wait for the LORD;
*   be strong and take heart*
*   and wait for the LORD.*

PSALM 27:14

As for me, I watch in hope for the LORD,
*   I wait for God my Savior;*
*   my God will hear me.*

MICAH 7:7

PATIENCE

I waited patiently for the LORD;
*   he turned to me and heard my cry.*
He lifted me out of the slimy pit,
*   out of the mud and mire;*
he set my feet on a rock
*   and gave me a firm place to stand.*

PSALM 40:1-2

A person's wisdom yields patience;
*   it is to one's glory to overlook an offense.*

PROVERBS 19:11

Fools show their annoyance at once,
*   but the prudent overlook an insult.*

PROVERBS 12:16

Whoever is patient has great understanding,
*   but one who is quick-tempered displays folly.*

PROVERBS 14:29

PEACE

Since we have been justified through faith,
we have peace with God through our Lord
Jesus Christ.

ROMANS 5:1

I will listen to what God the LORD says;
*   he promises peace to his people, his faithful*
*   servants.*

PSALM 85:8

Great peace have they who love your law,
*   and nothing can make them stumble.*

PSALM 119:165

You will keep in perfect peace
*   those whose minds are steadfast,*
*   because they trust in you.*

ISAIAH 26:3

In every situation, by prayer and petition, with
thanksgiving, present your requests to God.
And the peace of God, which transcends all
understanding, will guard your hearts and your
minds in Christ Jesus.

PHILIPPIANS 4:6-7

PEACE

The mind governed by the Spirit is life
and peace.

ROMANS 8:6

When the LORD takes pleasure in anyone's way,
he causes their enemies to make peace
with them.

PROVERBS 16:7

Peacemakers who sow in peace reap a harvest
of righteousness.

JAMES 3:18

"Blessed are the peacemakers,
for they will be called children of God."

MATTHEW 5:9

Finally, brothers and sisters, rejoice! Strive for
full restoration, encourage one another, be of
one mind, live in peace. And the God of love
and peace will be with you.

2 CORINTHIANS 13:11

PERSEVERANCE

Blessed is the one who perseveres under trial because, having stood the test, that person will receive the crown of life that the Lord has promised to those who love him.

JAMES 1:12

Stand firm. Let nothing move you. Always give yourselves fully to the work of the Lord, because you know that your labor in the Lord is not in vain.

1 CORINTHIANS 15:58

"I am coming soon. Hold on to what you have, so that no one will take your crown."

REVELATION 3:11

Be alert and of sober mind. Your enemy the devil prowls around like a roaring lion looking for someone to devour. Resist him, standing firm in the faith, because you know that the family of believers throughout the world is undergoing the same kind of sufferings.

1 PETER 5:8-9

PERSEVERANCE

*To those who by persistence in doing good
  seek glory, honor and immortality, he will
  give eternal life.*

ROMANS 2:7

*My steps have held to your paths;
  my feet have not stumbled.*

PSALM 17:5

Let perseverance finish its work so that you
may be mature and complete, not lacking
anything.

JAMES 1:4

Let us not become weary in doing good, for at
the proper time we will reap a harvest if we do
not give up.

GALATIANS 6:9

PRAISE

Praise the LORD, my soul,
    and forget not all his benefits—
who forgives all your sins
    and heals all your diseases.

PSALM 103:2-3

Praise be to the LORD,
    for he has heard my cry for mercy.

PSALM 28:6

For what you have done I will always
      praise you
    in the presence of your faithful people.
And I will hope in your name,
    for your name is good.

PSALM 52:9

PRAISE

You turned my wailing into dancing;
*   you removed my sackcloth and clothed me*
*   with joy,*
that my heart may sing your praises and not
*   be silent.*
LORD my God, I will give you praise forever.

PSALM 30:11-12

I keep my eyes always on the LORD.
*   With him at my right hand, I will not be*
*   shaken.*
Therefore my heart is glad and my tongue
*   rejoices;*
*   my body also will rest secure.*

PSALM 16:8-9

PRAYER

"If you remain in me and my words remain in you, ask whatever you wish, and it will be done for you."

JOHN 15:7

"If you believe, you will receive whatever you ask for in prayer."

MATTHEW 21:22

"Everyone who asks receives; one who seeks finds; and to the one who knocks, the door will be opened."

MATTHEW 7:8

"Until now you have not asked for anything in my name. Ask and you will receive, and your joy will be complete."

JOHN 16:24

I call on you, God, for you will answer me;
turn your ear to me and hear my prayer.

PSALM 17:6

PRAYER

If any of you lacks wisdom, you should ask God, who gives generously to all without finding fault, and it will be given to you.

JAMES 1:5

In the same way, the Spirit helps us in our weakness. We do not know what we ought to pray for, but the Spirit himself intercedes for us throught wordless groans.

ROMANS 8:26

"But I tell you, love your enemies and pray for those who persecute you, that you may be children of your Father in heaven. He causes his sun to rise on the evil and the good, and sends rain on the righteous and the unrighteous."

MATTHEW 5:44-45

Pray in the Spirit on all occasions with all kinds of prayers and requests. With this in mind, be alert and always keep on praying for all the Lord's people.

EPHESIANS 6:18

PRESENCE OF GOD

The LORD is near to all who call on him,
*   to all who call on him in truth.*

PSALM 145:18

Reach out for [God] and find him, though he
is not far from any one of us.

ACTS 17:27

If I rise on the wings of the dawn,
*   if I settle on the far side of the sea,*
even there your hand will guide me,
*   your right hand will hold me fast.*

PSALM 139:9-10

"Never will I leave you;
*   never will I forsake you."*

HEBREWS 13:5

Be strong and courageous. Do not be afraid or
terrified because of them, for the LORD your
God goes with you; he will never leave you nor
forsake you.

DEUTERONOMY 31:6

PRESENCE OF GOD

Even though I walk
through the darkest valley,
I will fear no evil,
for you are with me;
your rod and your staff,
they comfort me.

PSALM 23:4

"When you pass through the waters,
I will be with you;
and when you pass through the rivers,
they will not sweep over you.
When you walk through the fire,
you will not be burned;
the flames will not set you ablaze.
For I am the LORD, your God,
the Holy One of Israel, your Savior."

ISAIAH 43:2–3

The LORD replied, "My Presence will go with
you, and I will give you rest."

EXODUS 33:14

PRIORITIES

"Seek first his kingdom and his righteousness, and all these things will be given to you as well."

MATTHEW 6:33

Now all has been heard;
here is the conclusion of the matter:
Fear God and keep his commandments,
for this is the duty of all mankind.

ECCLESIASTES 12:13

We make it our goal to please him, whether we are at home in the body or away from it.

2 CORINTHIANS 5:9

"No one can serve two masters. Either you will hate the one and love the other, or you will be devoted to the one and despise the other. You cannot serve both God and money."

MATTHEW 6:24

Whoever pursues righteousness and love
finds life, prosperity and honor.

PROVERBS 21:21

PRIORITIES

Flee the evil desires of youth and pursue righteousness, faith, love and peace, along with those who call on the Lord out of a pure heart.

2 Timothy 2:22

Like newborn babies, crave pure spiritual milk, so that by it you may grow up in your salvation.

1 Peter 2:2

Forgetting what is behind and straining toward what is ahead, I press on toward the goal to win the prize for which God has called me heavenward in Christ Jesus.

Philippians 3:13-14

Jehoshaphat also said to the king of Israel, "First seek the counsel of the Lord."

1 Kings 22:5

PROTECTION

Cast your cares on the LORD
   and he will sustain you;
   he will never let the righteous be shaken.

PSALM 55:22

The LORD watches over all who love him,
   but all the wicked he will destroy.

PSALM 145:20

For the LORD loves the just
   and will not forsake his faithful ones.
Wrongdoers will be completely destroyed;
   the offspring of the wicked will perish.

PSALM 37:28

"Because he loves me," says the LORD, "I will
     rescue him;
   I will protect him, for he acknowledges
     my name.
He will call upon me, and I will answer him;
   I will be with him in trouble,
   I will deliver him and honor him."

PSALM 91:14-15

The eternal God is your refuge,
   and underneath are the everlasting arms.
He will drive out your enemies before you,
   saying, "Destroy him!"

DEUTERONOMY 33:27

PROTECTION

As for God, his way is perfect:
*   The LORD's word is flawless;*
*   he shields all who take refuge in him.*

2 SAMUEL 22:31

He holds victory in store for the upright,
*   he is a shield to those whose walk is*
*   blameless,*
for he guards the course of the just
*   and protects the way of his faithful ones.*

PROVERBS 2:7-8

You are my hiding place;
*   you will protect me from trouble*
*   and surround me with songs of deliverance.*

PSALM 32:7

The Lord is faithful, and he will strengthen
you and protect you from the evil one.

2 THESSALONIANS 3:3

PROVISION OF GOD

My God will meet all your needs according to the riches of his glory in Christ Jesus.

PHILIPPIANS 4:19

The LORD is my shepherd, I lack nothing.

PSALM 23:1

Be glad, people of Zion,
rejoice in the LORD your God,
for he has given you
the autumn rains because he is faithful.
He sends you abundant showers,
both autumn and spring rains, as before.

JOEL 2:23

[God] provides food for those who fear him;
he remembers his covenant forever.

PSALM 111:5

I will bless her with abundant provisions;
her poor will I satisfy with food.

PSALM 132:15

PROVISION OF GOD

[God] has shown kindness by giving you rain from heaven and crops in their seasons; he provides you with plenty of food and fills your hearts with joy.

ACTS 14:17

God is able to bless you abundantly, so that in all things at all times, having all that you need, you will abound in every good work.

2 CORINTHIANS 9:8

"Which of you, if your son asks for bread, will give him a stone? Or if he asks for a fish, will give him a snake? If you, then, though you are evil, know how to give good gifts to your children, how much more will your Father in heaven give good gifts to those who ask him!"

MATTHEW 7:9-11

PURPOSE

The Lord will vindicate me;
your love, Lord, endures forever—
do not abandon the works of your hands.

PSALM 138:8

We know that in all things God works for the good of those who love him, who have been called according to his purpose.

ROMANS 8:28

We are God's handiwork, created in Christ Jesus to do good works, which God prepared in advance for us to do.

EPHESIANS 2:10

Do not conform to the pattern of this world, but be transformed by the renewing of your mind. Then you will be able to test and approve what God's will is—his good, pleasing and perfect will.

ROMANS 12:2

PURPOSE

We constantly pray for you, that our God may make you worthy of his calling, and that by his power he may bring to fruition your every desire for goodness and your every deed prompted by faith.

2 THESSALONIANS 1:11

Because God wanted to make the unchanging nature of his purpose very clear to the heirs of what was promised, he confirmed it with an oath. God did this so that ... we who have fled to take hold of the hope set before to us may be greatly encouraged.

HEBREWS 6:17-18

It is God's will that by doing good you should silence the ignorant talk of foolish people.

1 PETER 2:15

In him we were also chosen, having been predestined according to the plan of him who works out everything in conformity with the purpose of his will, in order that we, who were the first to put our hope in Christ, might be for the praise of his glory.

EPHESIANS 1:11-12

QUIETNESS & REST

*I have calmed and quieted myself,
   I am like a weaned child with its mother;
   like a weaned child I am content.*

PSALM 131:2

*Be still before the LORD and wait patiently
   for him.*

PSALM 37:7

*The LORD will fight for you; you need only
   to be still.*

EXODUS 14:14

*"Be still, and know that I am God;
   I will be exalted among the nations,
   I will be exalted in the earth."*

PSALM 46:10

*Teach me, and I will be quiet;
   show me where I have been wrong.*

JOB 6:24

*"Take my yoke upon you and learn from me,
for I am gentle and humble in heart, and you
will find rest for your souls."*

MATTHEW 11:29

QUIETNESS & REST

"Come to me, all you who are weary and burdened, and I will give you rest. Take my yoke upon you and learn from me, for I am gentle and humble in heart, and you will find rest for your souls. For my yoke is easy and my burden is light."

MATTHEW 11:28-30

The fear of the LORD leads to life:
Then one rests content, untouched by trouble.

PROVERBS 19:23

In peace I will lie down and sleep,
for you alone, O LORD,
make me dwell in safety.

PSALM 4:8

Truly my soul finds rest in God;
my salvation comes from him.
Truly he is my rock and my salvation;
he is my fortress, I will never be shaken.

PSALM 62:1-2

REDEMPTION

Christ redeemed us from the curse of the law by becoming a curse for us, for it is written: "Cursed is everyone who is hung on a pole."

GALATIANS 3:13

You know that it was not with perishable things such as silver or gold that you were redeemed from the empty way of life handed down to you from your ancestors, but with the precious blood of Christ, a lamb without blemish or defect.

1 PETER 1:18-19

He did not enter by means of the blood of goats and calves; but he entered the Most Holy Place once for all by his own blood, thus obtaining eternal redemption.

HEBREWS 9:12

In [Jesus] we have redemption through his blood, the forgiveness of sins, in accordance with the riches of God's grace.

EPHESIANS 1:7

REDEMPTION

It is because of him that you are in Christ Jesus, who has become for us wisdom from God—that is, our righteousness, holiness and redemption.

1 Corinthians 1:30

He has rescued us from the dominion of darkness and brought us into the kingdom of the Son he loves, in whom we have redemption, the forgiveness of sins.

Colossians 1:13-14

You came near when I called you,
*   and you said, "Do not fear."*
You Lord, you took up my case;
*   you redeemed my life.*

Lamentations 3:57-58

"I have swept away your offenses like a cloud,
*   your sins like the morning mist.*
Return to me,
*   for I have redeemed you."*

Isaiah 44:22

REPENTANCE

Repent, then, and turn to God, so that your sins may be wiped out, that times of refreshing may come from the Lord.

ACTS 3:19

The Lord is not slow in keeping his promise, as some understand slowness. Instead he is patient with you, not wanting anyone to perish, but everyone to come to repentance.

2 PETER 3:9

"I tell you that in the same way there will be more rejoicing in heaven over one sinner who repents than over ninety-nine righteous persons who do not need to repent."

LUKE 15:7

"If a wicked person turns away from all the sins they have committed and keeps all my decrees and does what is just and right, that person will surely live; they will not die."

EZEKIEL 18:21

REPENTANCE

Let the wicked forsake their ways
and the unrighteous their thoughts.
Let them turn to the LORD, and he will have
mercy on them,
and to our God, for he will freely pardon.

ISAIAH 55:7

"If my people, who are called by my name, will humble themselves and pray and seek my face and turn from their wicked ways, then I will hear from heaven, and I will forgive their sin and will heal their land."

2 CHRONICLES 7:14

REWARD

*"I the L*ORD *search the heart*
and examine the mind,
to reward each person according to their
conduct,
according to what their deeds deserve."

JEREMIAH 17:10

*The L*ORD *has dealt with me according to my*
righteousness;
according to the cleanness of my hands he
has rewarded me.

PSALM 18:20

Whatever you do, work at it with all your heart, as working for the Lord, not for human masters, since you know that you will receive an inheritance from the Lord as a reward. It is the Lord Christ you are serving.

COLOSSIANS 3:23-24

Blessed is the one who perseveres under trial, because having stood the test, that person will receive the crown of life that the Lord has promised to those who love him.

JAMES 1:12

REWARD

"When you pray, go into your room, close the door and pray to your Father, who is unseen. Then your Father, who sees what is done in secret, will reward you."

MATTHEW 6:6

"Love your enemies, do good to them, and lend to them without expecting to get anything back. Then your reward will be great, and you will be children of the Most High, because he is kind to the ungrateful and wicked."

LUKE 6:35

"Look, I am coming soon! My reward is with me, and I will give to each person according to what they have done."

REVELATION 22:12

See, the Sovereign LORD comes with power,
and he rules with a mighty arm.
See, his reward is with him,
and his recompense accompanies him.

ISAIAH 40:10

RIGHTEOUSNESS

"Blessed are those who hunger and thirst for righteousness, for they will be filled."

MATTHEW 5:6

"*Sow for yourselves righteousness,*
    reap the fruit of unfailing love,
and break up your unplowed ground;
    for it is time to seek the LORD,
until he comes
    and showers righteousness on you."

HOSEA 10:12

The fruit of that righteousness will be peace;
    its the effect will be quietness and confidence
        forever.

ISAIAH 32:17

In the way of righteousness there is life;
    along that path is immortality.

PROVERBS 12:28

The eyes of the Lord are on the righteous and his ears are attentive to their prayer.

1 PETER 3:12

RIGHTEOUSNESS

Surely the righteous will never be shaken;
*   they will be remembered forever.*
They will have no fear of bad news;
*   their hearts are steadfast, trusting in the*
*   LORD.*

PSALM 112:6-7

The mouths of the righteous utter wisdom,
*   and their tongues speak what is just.*
The law of their God is in their hearts;
*   their feet do not slip.*

PSALM 37:30-31

Religion that God our Father accepts as pure
and faultless is this: to look after orphans and
widows in their distress and to keep oneself
from being polluted by the world.

JAMES 1:27

[God] does not take his eyes off the righteous;
*   he enthrones them with kings*
*   and exalts them forever.*

JOB 36:7

SALVATION

God our Savior ... wants all people to be saved
and to come to a knowledge of the truth.

1 TIMOTHY 2:3–4

[He] says,

"In the time of my favor I heard you,
and in the day of salvation I helped you."

I tell you, now is the time of God's favor,
now is the day of salvation.

2 CORINTHIANS 6:2

If you declare with your mouth, "Jesus is Lord,"
and believe in your heart that God raised him
from the dead, you will be saved.

ROMANS 10:9

All the prophets testify about [Jesus] that
everyone who believes in him receives
forgiveness of sins through his name.

ACTS 10:43

Once made perfect, [Jesus] became the source
of eternal salvation for all who obey him.

HEBREWS 5:9

SALVATION

"Whoever believes and is baptized will be saved, but whoever does not believe will be condemned."

MARK 16:16

He saved us, not because of righteous things we had done, but because of his mercy. He saved us through the washing of rebirth and renewal by the Holy Spirit.

TITUS 3:5

He lifted me out of the slimy pit,
*   out of the mud and mire;*
he set my feet on a rock
*   and gave me a firm place to stand.*

PSALM 40:2

SCRIPTURE

Jesus answered, "It is written: 'Man shall not live on bread alone, but on every word that comes from the mouth of God.'"

MATTHEW 4:4

The law of the LORD is perfect,
  refreshing the soul.
The statutes of the LORD are trustworthy,
  making wise the simple.

PSALM 19:7

Everything that was written in the past was written to teach us, so that through the endurance taught in the Scriptures and the encouragement they provide we might have hope.

ROMANS 15:4

The word of God is alive and active. Sharper than any double-edged sword, it penetrates even to dividing soul and spirit, joints and marrow; it judges the thoughts and attitudes of the heart.

HEBREWS 4:12

SCRIPTURE

All Scripture is God-breathed and is useful for teaching, rebuking, correcting and training in righteousness, so that the servant of God may be thoroughly equipped for every good work.

2 TIMOTHY 3:16-17

"Keep this Book of the Law always on your lips; meditate on it day and night, so that you may be careful to do everything written in it. Then you will be prosperous and successful."

JOSHUA 1:8

If you pay attention to these laws and are careful to follow them, then the LORD your God will keep his covenant of love with you, as he swore to your ancestors.

DEUTERONOMY 7:12

Great peace have those who love your law,
and nothing can make them stumble.

PSALM 119:165

SECURITY

Lord, you alone are my portion and my cup;
  you make my lot secure.

Psalm 16:5

"I will heal my people and will let them enjoy
abundant peace and security."

Jeremiah 33:6

"I give them eternal life, and they shall never
perish; no one will snatch them out of my
hand."

John 10:28

Those who know your name will trust in you,
  for you, Lord, have never forsaken those
    who seek you.

Psalm 9:10

Those who trust in the Lord are like
    Mount Zion,
  which cannot be shaken but endures forever.

Psalm 125:1

SECURITY

*I keep my eyes always on the L*ORD*.*
*   With him at my right hand, I will not be*
*   shaken.*

PSALM **16:8**

*Let the beloved of the L*ORD *rest secure in him,*
*   for he shields him all day long, and the*
*   one the L*ORD *loves rests between his*
*   shoulders.*

DEUTERONOMY **33:12**

We say with confidence,
"The Lord is my helper; I will not be afraid.
*   What can mere mortals do to me?"*

HEBREWS **13:6**

Who is going to harm you if you are eager to
do good?

1 PETER **3:13**

I am convinced that neither death nor life,
neither angels nor demons, neither the present
nor the future, nor any powers, neither height
nor depth, nor anything else in all creation,
will be able to separate us from the love of
God that is in Christ Jesus our Lord.

ROMANS **8:38–39**

SEEKING GOD

Seek the LORD while he may be found;
* call on him while he is near.*
Let the wicked forsake their ways
* and the unrighteous their thoughts.*
Let them turn to the LORD, and he will have
*   mercy on them,*
* and to our God, for he will freely pardon.*

ISAIAH 55:6-7

"You will call on me and come and pray
to me, and I will listen to you. You will seek
me and find me when you seek me with all
your heart. I will be found by you," declares
the LORD.

JEREMIAH 29:12-14

"Ask and it will be given to you; seek and you
will find; knock and the door will be opened to
you. For everyone who asks receives; the one
who seeks finds; and to the one who knocks,
the door will be opened."

LUKE 11:9-10

SEEKING GOD

Without faith it is impossible to please God, because anyone who comes to him must believe that he exists and that he rewards those who earnestly seek him.

HEBREWS 11:6

The LORD is good to those whose hope is
  in him,
  to the one who seeks him.

LAMENTATIONS 3:25

The LORD looks down from heaven
  on all mankind
to see if there are any who understand,
  any who seek God.

PSALM 14:2

Those who know your name trust in you, for you, LORD, have never forsaken those who seek you.

PSALM 9:10

If … you seek the LORD your God, you will find him if you seek him with all your heart and with all your soul.

DEUTERONOMY 4:29

SELF-CONTROL

Jesus said to his disciples, "Whoever wants to be my disciple must deny themselves and take up their cross and follow me."

MATTHEW 16:24

The grace of God has appeared that offers salvation to all people. It teaches us to say "No" to ungodliness and worldly passions, and to live self-controlled, upright and godly lives in this present age.

TITUS 2:11-12

Therefore, with minds that are alert and fully sober, set your hope on the grace to be brought to you when Jesus Christ is revealed at his coming.

1 PETER 1:13

The end of all things is near. Therefore be alert and of sober mind so that you may pray.

1 PETER 4:7

Let us be sober, putting on faith and love as a breastplate, and the hope of salvation as a helmet.

1 THESSALONIANS 5:8

SELF-CONTROL

"Watch and pray so that you will not fall into temptation. The spirit is willing, but the flesh is weak."

MATTHEW 26:41

Be alert and of sober mind. Your enemy the devil prowls around like a roaring lion looking for someone to devour.

1 PETER 5:8

If you live according to the flesh, you will die; but if by the Spirit you put to death the misdeeds of the body, you will live.

ROMANS 8:13

No temptation has overtaken you except what is common to mankind. And God is faithful; he will not let you be tempted beyond what you can bear. But when you are tempted, he will also provide a way out so that you can endure it.

1 CORINTHIANS 10:13

Because he himself suffered when he was tempted, he is able to help those who are being tempted.

HEBREWS 2:18

SELF-WORTH

*"Before I formed you in the womb I knew you,
  before you were born I set you apart."*

JEREMIAH 1:5

"Are not two sparrows sold for a penny? Yet
not one of them will fall to the ground outside
your Father's care. And even the very hairs of
your head are all numbered. So don't be afraid;
you are worth more than many sparrows."

MATTHEW 10:29-31

*"Since you are precious and honored in
      my sight,
    and because I love you,
I will give people in exchange for you,
    nations in exchange for your life."*

ISAIAH 43:4

*Know that the LORD is God.
    It is he who made us, and we are his;
    we are his people, the sheep of his pasture.*

PSALM 100:3

SELF-WORTH

You created my inmost being;
   you knit me together in my mother's womb.
I praise you because I am fearfully and
      wonderfully made;
   your works are wonderful,
   I know that full well.

PSALM 139:13-14

"Can a mother forget the baby at her breast
   and have no compassion on the child she
      has borne?
Though she may forget,
   I will not forget you!
See, I have engraved you on the palms of
      my hands;
   your walls are ever before me."

ISAIAH 49:15-16

[God] predestined us for adoption to sonship through Jesus Christ, in accordance with his pleasure and will—to the praise of his glorious grace, which he has freely given us in the One he loves.

EPHESIANS 1:5-6

SPEECH

*Those who guard their mouths and their tongues
keep themselves from calamity.*

PROVERBS 21:23

We all stumble in many ways. Anyone who is
never at fault in what they say is perfect, able
to keep their whole body in check.

JAMES 3:2

Do not let any unwholesome talk come out
of your mouths, but only what is helpful for
building others up according to their needs,
that it may benefit those who listen.

EPHESIANS 4:29

A gentle answer turns away wrath.

PROVERBS 15:1

*Whoever would love life
and see good days
must keep their tongue from evil
and their lips from deceitful speech.*

1 PETER 3:10

SPEECH

The soothing tongue is a tree of life,
but a perverse tongue crushes the spirit.

PROVERBS 15:4

Speaking the truth in love, we will grow to
become in every respect the mature body of
him who is the head, that is, Christ.

EPHESIANS 4:15

Gracious words are a honeycomb,
sweet to the soul and healing to the bones.

PROVERBS 16:24

Like apples of gold in settings of silver
is a ruling rightly given.

PROVERBS 25:11

The quiet words of the wise are more to be
heeded
than the shouts of a ruler of fools.

ECCLESIASTES 9:17

STABILITY

*I keep my eyes always on the L*ORD.
*With him at my right hand, I will not be
shaken.*

PSALM 16:8

*Strengthen the feeble hands,
steady the knees that give way;
say to those with fearful hearts,*
*"Be strong, do not fear;
your God will come."*

ISAIAH 35:3-4

*Truly my soul finds rest in God;
my salvation comes from him.
Truly he is my rock and my salvation;
he is my fortress, I will never be shaken.*

PSALM 62:1-2

The God of all grace, who called you to his
eternal glory in Christ, after you have suffered
a little while, will himself restore you and
make you strong, firm and steadfast.

1 PETER 5:10

STABILITY

To him who is able to keep you from stumbling and to present you before his glorious presence without fault and with great joy—to the only God our Savior be glory, majesty, power and authority, through Jesus Christ our Lord, before all ages, now and forevermore! Amen.

JUDE vv. 24–25

The LORD makes firm the steps
    of the one who delights in him;
though he may stumble, he will not fall,
    for the LORD upholds him with his hand.

PSALM 37:23–24

Whoever walks in integrity walks securely,
    but whoever takes crooked paths will be
        found out.

PROVERBS 10:9

Anyone who loves their brother and sister lives in the light, and there is nothing in them to make them stumble.

1 JOHN 2:10

STRENGTH

"Do not fear, for I am with you;
    do not be dismayed, for I am your God.
I will strengthen you and help you;
    I will uphold you with my righteous
        right hand."

ISAIAH 41:10

I can do all this through him who gives
me strength.

PHILIPPIANS 4:13

But [Jesus] said to me, "My grace is sufficient
for you, for my power is made perfect in
weakness." Therefore I will boast all the more
gladly about my weaknesses, so that Christ's
power may rest on me.

2 CORINTHIANS 12:9

My flesh and my heart may fail,
    but God is the strength of my heart
    and my portion forever.

PSALM 73:26

STRENGTH

It is God who arms me with strength
and keeps my way secure.
He makes my feet like the feet of a deer;
he causes me to stand on the heights.

2 SAMUEL 22:33-34

"I will search for the lost and bring back the
strays. I will bind up the injured and strengthen
the weak, but the sleek and the strong I will
destroy. I will shepherd the flock with justice."

EZEKIEL 34:16

[The LORD] gives strength to the weary
and increases the power of the weak.

ISAIAH 40:29

The LORD gives strength to his people;
the LORD blesses his people with peace.

PSALM 29:11

The LORD is my strength and my defense;
he has become my salvation.
He is my God, and I will praise him,
my father's God, and I will exalt him.

EXODUS 15:2

THANKFULNESS

Let the message of Christ dwell among you richly as you teach and admonish one another with all wisdom through psalms, hymns, and songs from the Spirit, singing to God with gratitude in your hearts.

COLOSSIANS 3:16

Let them give thanks to the LORD for his
    unfailing love
and his wonderful deeds for mankind,
for he satisfies the thirsty
    and fills the hungry with good things.

PSALM 107:8-9

Just as you received Christ Jesus as Lord, continue to live your lives in him, rooted and built up in him, strengthened in the faith as you were taught, and overflowing with thankfulness.

COLOSSIANS 2:6-7

Give thanks to the LORD, for he is good;
    his love endures forever.

1 CHRONICLES 16:34

THANKFULNESS

You turned my wailing into dancing;
  you removed my sackcloth and clothed me
    with joy,
that my heart may sing your praises and not
    be silent.
  *L*ORD *my God, I will praise you forever.*

PSALM 30:11-12

*The L*ORD *is my strength and my shield;*
  my heart trusts in him, and he helps me.
My heart leaps for joy,
  and with my song I praise him.

PSALM 28:7

Since we are receiving a kingdom that cannot
be shaken, let us be thankful, and so worship
God acceptably with reverence and awe.

HEBREWS 12:28

Give thanks in all circumstances, for this is
God's will for you in Christ Jesus.

1 THESSALONIANS 5:18

THOUGHTS

Finally, brothers and sisters, whatever is true, whatever is noble, whatever is right, whatever is pure, whatever is lovely, whatever is admirable—if anything is excellent or praiseworthy—think about such things.

PHILIPPIANS 4:8

Be transformed by the renewing of your mind. Then you will be able to test and approve what God's will is—his good, pleasing and perfect will.

ROMANS 12:2

We demolish arguments and every pretension that sets itself up against the knowledge of God, and we take captive every thought to make it obedient to Christ.

2 CORINTHIANS 10:5

The plans of the righteous are just,
but the advice of the wicked is deceitful.

PROVERBS 12:5

THOUGHTS

The LORD knows all human plans;
*   he knows that they are futile.*

PSALM 94:11

You will keep in perfect peace
*   those whose minds are steadfast,*
*   because they trust in you.*

ISAIAH 26:3

"I the LORD search the heart
*   and examine the mind,*
to reward each person according to their
*   conduct,*
*   according to what their deeds deserve."*

JEREMIAH 17:10

"Blessed are the pure in heart,
*   for they will see God."*

MATTHEW 5:8

The mind governed by the Spirit is life
and peace.

ROMANS 8:6

TRUST

*It is better to take refuge in the L*ORD
   than to trust in humans.

PSALM 118:8

"You believe in God; believe also in me."

JOHN 14:1

Blessed is the one
   *who trusts in the L*ORD,
who does not look to the proud,
   to those who turn aside to false gods.

PSALM 40:4

*This is what the Sovereign L*ORD, *the Holy One*
   of Israel, says:
   "In repentance and rest is your salvation,
in quietness and trust is your strength."

ISAIAH 30:15

TRUST

So this is what the Sovereign Lord *says:*
"See, I lay a stone in Zion, a tested stone,
  a precious cornerstone for a sure foundation;
the one who relies on it
  will never be stricken with panic."

Isaiah **28:16**

You will keep in perfect peace
  those whose minds are steadfast,
  because they trust in you.
Trust in the Lord *forever,*
  for the Lord*, the* Lord *himself, is the Rock*
    eternal.

Isaiah **26:3-4**

"Blessed is the one who trusts in the Lord*,*
  whose confidence is in him.
They will be like a tree planted by the water
  that sends out its roots by the stream.
It does not fear when heat comes;
  its leaves are always green.
It has no worries in a year of drought
  and never fails to bear fruit."

Jeremiah **17:7-8**

TRUTH

Kings take pleasure in honest lips;
*   they value the one who speaks what is right.*

PROVERBS 16:13

The LORD is near to all who call on him,
*   to all who call on him in truth.*

PSALM 145:18

Jesus answered, "I am the way and the truth
and the life. No one comes to the Father
except through me."

JOHN 14:6

Jesus said, "If you hold to my teaching, you are
really my disciples. Then you will know the
truth, and the truth will set you free."

JOHN 8:31-32

We know also that the Son of God has come
and has given us understanding, so that we
may know him who is true. And we are in him
who is true by being in his Son Jesus Christ.
He is the true God and eternal life.

1 JOHN 5:20

TRUTH

"When he, the Spirit of truth, comes, he will guide you into all the truth. He will not speak on his own; he will speak only what he hears, and he will tell you what is yet to come."

JOHN 16:13

Buy the truth and do not sell it —
wisdom, instruction and insight as well.

PROVERBS 23:23

All your words are true;
all your righteous laws are eternal.

PSALM 119:160

I am about to go the way of all the earth. You know with all your heart and soul that not one of all the good promises the LORD your God gave you has failed. Every promise has been fulfilled; not one has failed.

JOSHUA 23:14

VICTORY

Thanks be to God! He gives us the victory through our Lord Jesus Christ.

1 Corinthians 15:57

"I have told you these things, so that in me you may have peace. In this world you will have trouble. But take heart! I have overcome the world."

John 16:33

Everyone born of God overcomes the world. This is the victory that has overcome the world, even our faith. Who is it that overcomes the world? Only the one who believes that Jesus is the Son of God.

1 John 5:4-5

The God of peace will soon crush Satan under your feet. The grace of our Lord Jesus be with you.

Romans 16:20

With God we will gain the victory,
and he will trample down our enemies.

Psalm 60:12

VICTORY

You, dear children, are from God and have overcome them, because the one who is in you is greater than the one who is in the world.

1 JOHN 4:4

In all these things we are more than conquerors through him who loved us.

ROMANS 8:37

When the perishable has been clothed with the imperishable, and the mortal with immortality, then the saying that is written will come true: "Death has been swallowed up in victory."

1 CORINTHIANS 15:54

There is no wisdom, no insight, no plan
*   that can succeed against the LORD.*
The horse is made ready for the day of battle,
*   but victory rests with the LORD.*

PROVERBS 21:30-31

For lack of guidance a nation falls,
*   but victory is won through many advisers.*

PROVERBS 11:14

WILL OF GOD

The world and its desires pass away, but whoever does the will of God lives forever.

1 John 2:17

Be transformed by the renewing of your mind. Then you will be able to test and approve what God's will is—his good, pleasing and perfect will.

Romans 12:2

[God] made known to us the mystery of his will according to his good pleasure, which he purposed in Christ, to be put into effect when the times reach their fulfillment—to bring unity to all things in heaven and on earth under Christ.

Ephesians 1:9-10

Grace and peace to you from God our Father and the Lord Jesus Christ, who gave himself for our sins to rescue us from the present evil age, according to the will of our God and Father, to whom be glory for ever and ever. Amen.

Galatians 1:3-5

WILL OF GOD

In him we were also chosen, having been predestined according to the plan of him who works out everything in conformity with the purpose of his will, in order that we, who were the first to put our hope in Christ, might be for the praise of his glory.

EPHESIANS 1:11-12

"My Father's will is that everyone who looks to the Son and believes in him shall have eternal life, and I will raise them up at the last day."

JOHN 6:40

It is God's will that you should be sanctified: that you should avoid sexual immorality; that each of you should learn to control your own body in a way that is holy and honorable.

1 THESSALONIANS 4:3-4

Rejoice always, pray continually, give thanks in all circumstances; for this is God's will for you in Christ Jesus.

1 THESSALONIANS 5:16-18

WISDOM

*The fear of the LORD is the beginning
    of wisdom;
    all who follow his precepts have good
    understanding.
To him belongs eternal praise.*

PSALM 111:10

For the foolishness of God is wiser than human
wisdom, and the weakness of God is stronger
than human strength.

1 CORINTHIANS 1:25

If any of you lacks wisdom, you should ask
God, who gives generously to all without
finding fault, and it will be given to you.

JAMES 1:5

*The beginning of wisdom is this: Get wisdom.
    Though it cost all you have, get
    understanding.*

PROVERBS 4:7

*Know also that wisdom is like honey for you;
    if you find it, there is a future hope for you,
    and your hope will not be cut off.*

PROVERBS 24:14

WISDOM

*Wisdom, like an inheritance, is a good thing
and benefits those who see the sun.
Wisdom is a shelter
as money is a shelter,
but the advantage of knowledge is this:
Wisdom preserves those who have it.*

ECCLESIASTES 7:11-12

*How much better to get wisdom than gold,
to get insight rather than silver!*

PROVERBS 16:16

*Wisdom makes one wise person more powerful
than ten rulers in a city.*

ECCLESIASTES 7:19

The wisdom that comes from heaven is first
of all pure; then peace-loving, considerate,
submissive, full of mercy and good fruit,
impartial and sincere.

JAMES 3:17

WITNESSING

How beautiful on the mountains
    are the feet of those who bring good news,
who proclaim peace,
    who bring good tidings,
    who proclaim salvation,
who say to Zion,
    "Your God reigns!"

ISAIAH 52:7

Jesus came to them and said, "All authority in heaven and on earth has been given to me. Therefore go and make disciples of all nations, baptizing them in the name of the Father and of the Son and of the Holy Spirit, and teaching them to obey everything I have commanded you. And surely I am with you always, to the very end of the age."

MATTHEW 28:18-20

He said to them, "Go into all the world and preach the gospel to all creation."

MARK 16:15

WITNESSING

It is written: "I believed; therefore I have spoken." Since we have that same spirit of faith, we also believe and therefore speak.

2 Corinthians 4:13

He is the one we proclaim, admonishing and teaching everyone with all wisdom, so that we may present everyone fully mature in Christ.

Colossians 1:28

Do this with gentleness and respect, keeping a clear conscience, so that those who speak maliciously against your good behavior in Christ may be ashamed of their slander.

1 Peter 3:15-16

"In the same way, let your light shine before others, that they may see your good deeds and glorify your Father in heaven."

Matthew 5:16

"This gospel of the kingdom will be preached in the whole world as a testimony to all nations, and then the end will come."

Matthew 24:14

WORK

"Do not work for food that spoils, but for food that endures to eternal life, which the Son of Man will give you. For on him God the Father has placed his seal of approval."

JOHN 6:27

Stand firm. Let nothing move you. Always give yourselves fully to the work of the Lord, because you know that your labor in the Lord is not in vain.

1 CORINTHIANS 15:58

Never be lacking in zeal, but keep your spiritual fervor, serving the Lord.

ROMANS 12:11

Our people must learn to devote themselves to doing what is good, in order to provide for urgent needs and not live unproductive lives.

TITUS 3:14

WORK

This is what I have observed to be good: that it is appropriate for a person to eat, to drink and to find satisfaction in their toilsome labor under the sun during the few days of life God has given them—for this is their lot.

ECCLESIASTES 5:18

Diligent hands bring wealth.

PROVERBS 10:4

The desires of the diligent are fully satisfied.

PROVERBS 13:4

The sleep of a laborer is sweet,
*   whether they eat little or much,*
but as for the rich, their abundance
*   permits them no sleep.*

ECCLESIASTES 5:12

There remains, then, a Sabbath-rest for the people of God; for anyone who enters God's rest also rests from their works, just as God did from his.

HEBREWS 4:9-10